MY FAVORITE BIBLE STORIES
COLOR-BY-NUMBER COLORING BOOK

Written by: Robin Fogle
Illustrated by: Thomson Digital

Warner
Press Kids™
educate • nurture • inspire
www.warnerpress.org

NOAH'S ARK

God told Noah to build an ark. Noah took his family and two of every kind of animal
into the ark. For forty days the rain came down. The whole earth was flooded.
When the flood was over, God put a rainbow in the sky to remind us
of His promise never to flood the whole earth again.

1= red   2= blue   3= green   4= yellow   5= orange   6= purple   7= brown   8= black

JOSEPH & HIS COLORFUL COAT

Joseph's father, Jacob, had many sons but he loved Joseph most of all.
He gave Joseph a special coat to wear. This made Joseph's brothers jealous.
They sold Joseph as a slave, but God had great plans for him.
One day he would help his family and many other people.

1= red   2= blue   3= green   4= yellow   5= orange   6= purple   7= brown   8= black

BABY MOSES

A bad Pharaoh wanted the Hebrew baby boys to be killed. One mother wanted to save her baby. She put him in a basket and placed it in the river. Soon Pharaoh's daughter came for a bath and found the baby. She named him Moses and kept him for her son. When Moses grew up he led God's people away from Pharaoh to a new land.

1= red   2= blue   3= green   4= yellow   5= orange   6= purple   7= brown   8= black

SAMSON

God wanted Samson to help His people so He made him very strong. One time Samson fought and killed a lion with his bare hands. Samson liked to tell riddles but they always got him into trouble. Finally, he was tricked and his strength was gone. But God did not forget Samson. God made him strong one last time and all of his enemies were killed.

1= red   2= blue   3= green   4= yellow   5= orange   6= purple   7= brown   8= black

RUTH

Ruth wanted to return to Bethlehem with her mother-in-law Naomi. When they got there Ruth worked hard in the fields to find food. Boaz, the owner of the field, saw her and loved her. They got married and had a son. Naomi took care of little Obed, and everyone praised God for the way He had blessed them.

1= red   2= blue   3= green   4= yellow   5= orange   6= purple   7= brown   8= black

SAMUEL

When Hannah prayed for a baby God sent her Samuel. She took him to the temple to live and serve God. One night Samuel heard a voice calling him. He thought it was Eli the priest. Eli knew the voice was God. He told Samuel what to say, and God gave Samuel an important message. Samuel became a prophet and served God all of his life.

1= red   2= blue   3= green   4= yellow   5= orange   6= purple   7= brown   8= black

DAVID & GOLIATH

Goliath was yelling at God's army and all of the soldiers were afraid.
David, a young shepherd boy, told the king he would fight the giant.
With one small stone, a sling and God's help, David killed the giant.
Because David trusted God, God later made him king over His people.

1= red   2= blue   3= green   4= yellow   5= orange   6= purple   7= brown   8= black

ESTHER

When the king married Esther he did not know she was a Jew. Evil Haman convinced the king to order all the Jews to be killed. Esther had to be brave if she was going to save her people. She prayed to God then went to the king. When she told the king about Haman's plan he was angry. He ordered Haman to be killed and all the Jews were saved.

1= red   2= blue   3= green   4= yellow   5= orange   6= purple   7= brown   8= black

THREE MEN IN THE FURNACE

The king made a huge gold statue and told the people they had to bow down to it. Shadrach, Meshach and Abednego loved God. They would not bow down, so the king had them thrown into a hot, fiery furnace. When he looked in the furnace he saw an angel with the men. Then the three men came out of the furnace and they didn't even smell like smoke.

1= red   2= blue   3= green   4= yellow   5= orange   6= purple   7= brown   8= black

DANIEL & THE LIONS' DEN

Daniel broke the king's law by praying to God. The king had Daniel thrown into the lions' den. All night he worried about Daniel. In the morning he ran to the den and called to Daniel. Daniel told him that an angel had shut the lions' mouths so they could not hurt him. Then the king told everyone they should serve God from now on.

1= red   2= blue   3= green   4= yellow   5= orange   6= purple   7= brown   8= black

JONAH

God wanted Jonah to preach to the people of Ninevah. Jonah didn't want to go.
He ran away and got on a ship, but a bad storm came. The sailors had to throw
Jonah overboard. Jonah was swallowed by a huge fish. After three days and nights,
Jonah prayed and told God he would obey. Then the fish spit Jonah on dry land.

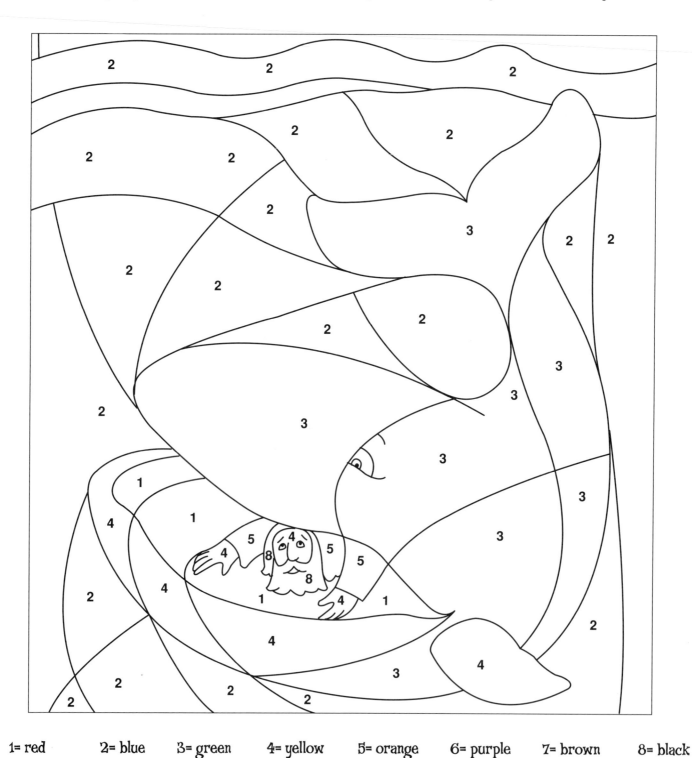

1= red   2= blue   3= green   4= yellow   5= orange   6= purple   7= brown   8= black

JESUS IS BORN

God chose a young girl named Mary to be the mother of His Son. Mary and her husband, Joseph, went to a little town called Bethlehem. There in a stable Jesus was born. Mary wrapped Him in soft cloths and laid Him in a manger. Angels told some shepherds the wonderful news. They were all so glad that Jesus was born!

1= red   2= blue   3= green   4= yellow   5= orange   6= purple   7= brown   8= black

JESUS FEEDS THE FIVE THOUSAND

Jesus had been teaching the people for a long time. No one had eaten all day.
Jesus told the disciples to feed the people but they had no food. A little boy gave them
five loaves of bread and two fish. Jesus blessed the food and the disciples passed it out.
When all the people had eaten, the disciples gathered 12 baskets of leftovers.

1= red   2= blue   3= green   4= yellow   5= orange   6= purple   7= brown   8= black

ZACCHAEUS

Zacchaeus was a rich tax collector. When Jesus came to town Zacchaeus was too short to see over the crowd. He climbed up in a tree and Jesus saw him there. Jesus told him to come down because He wanted to go to his house. Zacchaeus believed in Jesus and promised to give back even more money than he had taken from the people.

1= red   2= blue   3= green   4= yellow   5= orange   6= purple   7= brown   8= black

JESUS IS RISEN

Jesus died on the cross to save us from our sins. Then His body was put in a tomb.
Three days later some of Jesus' friends came to the tomb. The stone was rolled away!
The women saw an angel who told them that Jesus had risen.
Then they ran to tell the disciples the good news. Jesus is alive!

1= red   2= blue   3= green   4= yellow   5= orange   6= purple   7= brown   8= black

E465